KALEIDOSCOPES

By the same author:

Surface (2004)
I Think We Have (2007)
angles of a broken hill (Ed.) (2008)
Eye to Eye (2012)
For Instance (2015)
The Love of the Sun (2018)

KALEIDOSCOPES

MATT HETHERINGTON

RECENT
WORK
PRESS

Kaleidoscopes
Recent Work Press
Canberra, Australia

Copyright © Matt Hetherington, 2020

ISBN: 9780648834359 (paperback)

 A catalogue record for this book is available from the National Library of Australia

All rights reserved. This book is copyright. Except for private study, research, criticism or reviews as permitted under the Copyright Act, no part of this book may be reproduced, stored in a retrieval system, or transmitted in any form by any means without prior written permission. Enquiries should be addressed to the publisher.

Cover image: 'Illuminated Tunnel' by Simon Mann © 2020. Reproduced with permission.
Cover design: Recent Work Press
Set by Recent Work Press
Author photograph by Nigel Wells

recentworkpress.com

SS

For Marie Craven

Contents

ESCAPE

Outside In	3
Solace	4
C	5
Give It Up	6
Leaks	7
Light Ghazal	8
Skies	9
Less	10
P	11
Coal	12
Wasn't Listening	13
L	14
Night-Owl Lullaby	15
My Daughter at Eighty Months	16
Like	17
Minimal Characters	18
Oldie	19
Deep	20
Coda-9	21
Nothing	22
Deal	23
Copies Sold	24
Odalisk	25
I am at 1 a.m	26
Lies	27
Another Day	28
Mandatory	29
P.S	30
Indefinitely Thinker Paces Cage	31
Poesies	32
Sic [sic]	33
A	34

SAD	35
O	36
Solo	37
E	38
Smoke & Ash	39
Passed	40
Sepia	41
Don't	42
Eclipse	43
Fourteen Paces	44
The Dark	46

COLLIDE

The Dark Site	51
Four Paces	52
Specks	54
We Were Made	55
Loses	56
Please Do	57
Episodes	58
Loose Ideas	59
My Daughter at One Hundred Months	60
K	61
Dole	62
D	63
Seidel's	64
Polis	65
Close	66
Id	67
Repeat After Me	68
Adolesce	69
Lies	70
KID D	71
Idol	72
Solid Case	73

Thank You for Letting Me Be Someone Else Again	74
If You Go Away	75
Disclose	76
Clap	77
Disease	78
Minimal Characters	79
When I Knew	80
Speed	81
Sacked	82
Cool	83
Docile	84
A-Sides	85
How Low Now	86
Oops	87
As	88
Tough Thought Throughout Though	89
Space	90
Dick	91
I	92
OK	93
Inside Out	94
Afterword	95

'the kaleidoscope you looked better through'

Bronwen Manger, *'Half My Crimes'*

'If therefore thine eye be single, thy whole body shall be full of light.'

Matt. 6:22

ESCAPE

'before we can escape // we must remember to imprison ourselves'

Nathan Shepherdson, 'the easiest way to open a door is turn the handle'

Outside In

turns it round and around
to get inside out

turns off
on the outside

to get itself
off on itself

turns inside to get
outside itself

Solace

the sun, once again, has done its still
dance, and i sit in my little sweet
mansion on the hill, gazing over
the fields and the pale houses below me.

whatever it was that was wrong is not
in this room, or, it seems, in this street
where i have arrived, some sort
of mildly triumphant survivor.

i am the governor of this hand
and the possessor of a regal posture,
plus a sturdy old table of fine dark wood—
what does it matter what type of timber,
or whether i deserve this very good fortune?
it's enough that we both care about each other.

C

a heel and an eyeball
    lightning in the distance
around the corner is a street
                  brick-colour
      new bruises of too many crucial little things
      the floor of devotion
    as vast as the past
let it kill me, let it come like these many warm nights alone
      all walls fall
    chant it
      the emptiness of angels and enemies
there's no need to kiss seaweed
      recite your warnings quietly
in the autumn gloom, the false yawns of woe
    winds around my home like the sound of applause
last night the moon left something unshatterable behind
    a thumping fist of flesh inside the chest
plus a million visions of the seen
      first is last
    chant it
      as the sea breathes in and out
a heart parts
    silence louder than a star
        i swallowed your shadow
    our reward is more doors
make love, take leave

Give It Up

       i moisten my fingers with the vortex
then over and again i scrape my teeth along the length of the nape of your neck
         then i send you away so i can sigh about you being gone

           of course i soon grow lonely
                 so i beg you to come back and offer me
            the animal fruit that kisses my mouth

i like to lick in anti-clockwise circles
      then i linger
           in the scented desert that lies between your breasts

         i know your streets and retreats, your alleys and valleys
           and the perfumes that your flesh exudes
             when your spirit is being pleased

              now i try my best to give up
          these lightning bolts of love within me
         and to make books where the pages open like lips

Leaks

six months in a weak boat
lucky to be so alive
and alone enough to speak

no anchor for the huge
chill waters
of my own private isolake

can i even conceive
of one blacker than geneva
with all those ugly spirits
loaded up in the hills

not hard to find
who made you hide
for two whole seasons
like the hour before light

Light Ghazal

For Andy Jackson

the most overused word in poetry is 'light',
but what's inside sorrow's black marrow, if not light?

just don't try asking the hidden torturer, or
the prisoner condemned to nights of endless light.

though evil's everywhere, i refuse to forget
candles in darkness, and the glassiness of light.

true, dreams of suicide are a safe place to hide,
but wherever you end, it's still the same old light.

we're building temples to ourselves, and we want to
stay longer, but we're only making light of light.

when i look, what i'm seeking is vision past here,
and revolving mandalas of truth-coloured light,

so what's wrong with believing in shadows on screens
to transform the guilt of a burden that's too light?

matt, you can't hear curses or see blood on your hands,
but you're running away from and into it, light.

Skies

talk to me like i care
and they're correct
as i come a bit undone
when i look properly
or at least deeply then
i am liable to make
errors in life like
trying to say how it is
inside when touched
in such a way
the spirit spins on itself
or you can even
find them in tubes

Less

because there is more room
                for dream
because i need to pretend
      i'm modest
because even books
              kill trees
because of course
      you have better things to do
because life is too
      short too
            i love
                  you too

P

no matter what i mutter, you will know
   me by its silences

       getting it's not easier than it seems
but my drug is the floor in the rug

     maybe how a goat warbles
and our limited infinities play about the air

  or like how no one likes liking anymore, preferring
to publicly cross off items or support

the less poets put down, the more they say
    feel my sloth!

been licking my own forearms since i was four
     plus a review opined i 'speak good painish'

to read in place of writing
to sleep instead of dreaming

the future is a lot of white noise about regret
   with an absence of reparation

the great rains are coming
       i believe i must be grieving

Coal

'The cage opens. The canary closes its eyes.'
David Stavanger, 'Everyday Magician'

the canary sings like a canary.
it dreams of flying through the morning without moving;
its claws clutch at the perch,
but it's the yellow light only that rushes past,
and it sits almost still, tasting no things.

within the hardness of the coalmine's everyday heart
it falls into sleep with its little beak open,
seeing only caves of night
which suddenly bloom into fields of yellow air.
it chatters of false dawns in the lives of happy families
which sound like early-morning warnings;
it rises like a puff of cigarette smoke,
and drifts over crumpled fields and the need to wake up;
it skims over seas of yellow clouds
inside which perhaps are sleeping the hooded dead.

a drop drips from the ceiling.
a candle flickers in the draught the open door left.
someone has left the gas going.
gravity is holding on.

the canary sings like a canary.
the cage closes.
the canary opens its eyes.

Wasn't Listening

& you weren't with me either
& we rehearsed our insertions

& waited for something objectionable
& went on like that for quite a while

& then we got worn down
& couldn't hear anyway

& all we had was ourselves
& so much more we couldn't recall

L

she lights
a flame
in me that
smokes in
straight lines
up into my
fingers and i
have to move
them like the
fine dancer
i am in my
fancy jokes
that only she
smiles at
and she bares
her soul
through her
teeth and
the sacred
sight of her
eyes closing
so her   intellect
can go   off   into
outer reaches   of brighter dark   is more   than enough
to make   me unable   to separate   him from her

Night-Owl Lullaby

where are you right now, absent one?
what are your dark and peerless eyes lighting upon?

perhaps half of you is laughing,
or talking with a friend i might not know,
but another part is silent,
and needs my voice alone.

you and i are weary of the same old deceits;
we both want the peace our loneliness seeks.

so when you lie your tired head down
to dream some art tonight,
your heart will remind you
of your fear of the light.

and you will sense a deeper self
that waits at rest above you,
and you will sleep then,
and forget for a while that i love you.

My Daughter at Eighty Months

and now that i am gone
from where she lives, already
i'm losing things and missing things,
and it would seem that it's still alright,
but now that she is gone
from her five-week break with me,
and definitely truly
missed her mother after a month,
i sense that this most probably will be
the last time for a long time
we will ever be so close.

at least i have made her happy,
because this is the first time for years
she has seen me really happy myself,
since i am more gone on a woman
than i have been since before
she was born, and i believe
that she can see that joyousness,
and isn't that one of the best things
i can show her, other than the love
i feel for her, even though right here
most of this is really all about me?

Like

i like to forget
where i am

to see the sights
not as things
but as lights

to move smoothly
along the air itself

i like to be
without likes

to wake up
in my bed alone

to take my time
before meeting others
a little like me

Minimal Characters

the moronic coroner

the one in thrall to hunger

the blood-drinking child

the one swinging from the chandelier

the soldier afloat in the moat

the lady who only understands furry things

the shivering martyr

the one-eyed voyeur

the one with no habits

the one who is smug like some pug-ugly mug

the unemployed judge

the man who mistook his wife for a life

the one too tired to lie

the one who makes you beg for less

Oldie

never knew anyone better
at not speaking

or saying the opposite
of what he said

or letting the other bloke
tell what he wanted to hide

or even letting the silence
say the truth best

or at least better
than what he knows he could

it's as slow
as watching wood grow

Deep

venetians are closing
        on another small day
and you can see
    i'm complicated like a conquered face
        keep on keeping on and
round things roll off each other then sink
      wishes come out like cockroaches
that's midnight for you to dig
   i'd climb out of this hole but i can't feel the sides
no
   that's really something
                animal
          moaning like a crane
or my drizzle-soaked innards
om
   all windows and no doors
             no barge-arse though
   i swear with my nerves
a resisted bubble
          frightened by ventriloquists
and caught up in the beige apocalypse again
          sigh
   i keep forgetting i'm the universe too

Coda-9

after the deluge
it's me again
kneeling at the foot of the bed
for a change

still trying it out
there where i believe i belong

not a lost one but a lone one
like one being dreamt
or as a force remains in the core
of all the growing worlds

Nothing

nothing happened, is still happening, says 'i need you'
like crying peacock-drops on another screen you've come up against
where one's escaping out of something more comfortable
into staring at a pastime which had
touchy hindsight, you feel me?
please care, these normalizing drugs are banging
into my centering—you get a hot
peace-talk pole in your head, but why
waste a line with space?
each week wears the bruise of the one that went
the day before, and even though i live
a lifestyle to die for, and a wink
is a long time in politics, i'm past it
like a garnish of parsley on a seafood extender
true, we could put off procrastination
or each other—but i mean, hey
if you loved me, i promise
i'd be proud as a leader

Deal

he hated her least when she was walking away
only liked her because she left him alone
but everyone knows the lost ones often lie

they paid too much for just one large mistake
but the deal was always right there in the room
she hated him most when he was walking away

until it got late, he sulked and cooked each day
he had eight fine fingers working to the bone
but everyone knows us lost ones often lie

he knew he was deaf to what she wouldn't say
his fifteen best friends never answered their phones
she hated him least when she was walking away

she kept the car, he kept staring at the sky
he got sprung out of jail when it wasn't a home
but everyone knows the lost ones often lie

she couldn't face the truth and he couldn't cry
their love was left like an unfinished poem
he hated her most when he was walking away
but everyone knows us lost ones often lie

Copies Sold

that son of a nun was there again, but this time he was only watching. there were cobwebs over the front door, and i put my feet on the wrong way. the kitchen returned to where it was meant to be, and my stomach stayed in for the evening. the evening went out. don't know where it went, but it came home smelling pretty good. your derrière was nothing like a mosquito. i couldn't stop so i don't. she didn't let it bother her so something else did. a leaf drifted back to the branch.

one afternoon, we will find we are all folded over like magazines and newspapers, and someone will throw us in the corner, and after that more of us will be piled on top until eventually something has to be done about it. the corvids will grow bigger and darker, and the water will taste like mammals, but that will be ok. you will decode me, and still i won't be understood. i will understand. the critics will ignore us, and it will feel really critical. i will waste a night, but it won't be a waste.

there will be another conversation.

Odalisk

          the scent of your sex in the room
and when at last that is gone
i can pretend i will never
              have to taste you again

this dream of your death
        it keeps me breathing
    when it's only you
             who lets me live

I am at 1 a.m

    a lamb, though still the son of a sun, somewhat similar
to you, so pay attention for just a minute in order to get what's free
you think you can pick and choose like the world is your nose
    but you're stuck on the same page as me
        anyone would think i was a joker

    because, ok, i've had a few, so let me tell you
   as if you didn't get it, i'm spineless like a heart
but i'm an old soul, so hold your young tongue
    'ego' is not a flirty word
they know me well at the turn off to hell
    though i always go back to my bed

    this dude here, he's a silver ghost surfing the faces
in the calm between storms, dribbling on in the eye of morning
    as modern as a hall of mirrors, though he'd rather think
he was as large as the teachers abiding on the beaches of far distant
galaxies
    here and now, we're like live human flesh on special in supermarkets
        each of us out of reach of us
stumbling iambically in limbo, dancing away from the dark

Lies

        this will make you feel better

somewhere there's a country where the leader has no bodyguards

                the phrase 'we all believe'

    you complete me

imperfect symmetry is another original sin

        it makes no difference where you spend your money

    a thousand words are worth a picture

            all moments are not movements

you can bury your love in the meadow

            art is a luxury

        if i had paws, i could love you

        oh this and that

    because the heart is a bird it must stay in its cage

you need to know this

Another Day

without speaking, without laughing
   without my daughter
      or my brothers, or my father

         nobody else's body
            and no love
               other than what which i offer myself

                  a day without belief
                     but with the faith that what's needed
                     will be present, or return

                        a day of easily managed pains
                           of no alcohol or chocolate
                              but enough money for both if i want

                           a day with more than enough sunshine
                              and an abundance of others'
                              beautiful music and exquisite thought

                  another day of superb vegetables
                     and genuine fruit and bread and nuts
                     and the unending magnificence of lentils

         a day without tenderness or endearments
            but plenty of quiet smiling, and the exact
         right amount of easy, contented rest

Mandatory

the first have the worst thirst
wanting to set fire to a flame
no i've had so much i'm full
there's just too many people
do not like or copy and paste
it only makes us more alone
the neighbours almost silent
to die of it on the open ocean
some guy says let's get it on
as a dog moans up at the sun
they'll get a fair go in prison
who decides who comes here
for anger and stranger danger
each hell's unique as a home
you won't feel me or a thing
that's the way the cock flops
really only the lie of the land

P.S

'...and instigate new worlds, the traces of eternity.'
Ali Alizadeh, 'P.S'

everything in some
                familiar sense's what comes after that
          before doing this, but in between many old realms
      my mother lighting another cigarette, outside below zero
that other season you learned too late to trust in anything but dust
     that you live by the word, and will die by the word
the way the lost get found though
          days and nights to allow a low
                    she loved me like a goldfish
      each heart a tank, each head a blinking light
            dreaming of songs or open mouths
   a jackal never changes its spots
             rubbing your eyes won't help
  when i felt i could, i made it out alive
  the only thing i ever hit was the road
  now she is taking her revenge as she should
i am trying, and i smile like this with you
                a bird flies through an airport

Indefinitely Thinker Paces Cage

An Anagrammatic Response to Paul Valéry

*'The thinker is locked in a cage and paces
indefinitely between four words.'*

here is ink, and the key that hangs
in air like an infinite thread
there is archetypal death
and the dark honey needing lips

the thinker chases space, tinkers, dreams
then plays an early, defiant hand
each faces their dicey age, and learns
the escape that lies inside seeds

at peace, they find a degenerate idea
clear, stately, and freeing
and their transcendental typing ends easily
in dense and nearly perfect silence

Poesies

'Any action which is the cause of a thing emerging from non-existence into existence might be called poetry, and all the processes in all the crafts are kinds of poetry...'
Plato, Symposium, #205e

if there are to be fine layers, it helps if the outer one is tough

    these mirrors almost move themselves

          every orgy needs a scapegoat

    alright, i liked the poems less than the bios

      like air, it's all about me, after all

          you have to give, you don't have to live

art doesn't always agree with me, but i like to argue

      there are no beautiful words, only beautiful minds

everything's been said, but not everything's been heard

          there is less pleasure in being loved than loving

      remember who we never were?

Sic [sic]

yeah, i ate the mouse's head, but the cameras didn't SEE it,
       and i was in need of LIPS, though not those COPIED
ones, LIKE how killer sharks always LOOK LIKE
            they're smiling, SO go ASK ALICE, she goes
                'the suburbs are slaughterhouses for sheep', AS if
we're not standing around like a PACK of welders' dogs ourselves, but where
    are you supposed to LOOK when a DOSE of the CODE
         gets you LOCKED up again, and all the COP can DO
      is go 'PAL, nuffing fucken fitz n evryfingz in bitz'...huh? huh?

the POLICE are SICK, every man and his POLE knows that

    we just KEEP COOL, mind our PEAS, and make DEALS,
you got me? KEEP it how we both LIKE it,
                      nice LIKE ICE on a COLD one, right?
i'm no ALCO, though i've done some hard yards, yeah,
           but the truth IS
     even though i'm AS rare AS rocking-horse shit, bro,
i'm just LIKE you—you don't listen and i'm not talking
           i got my fingers in my ears until i drown, OK?
              now be a good boy and be gone like a woebegone wobbegong

A

Dali

i love to wank looking at myself
& when i do i give my seed over
to the ants of the earth or maybe
truly to posterity where it droops
forever into the yawning mouths
of billionaires who know better
than to expect to grow up or love

Picasso

i like to drink thinking of myself
& when i'm not i paint things to
stop me thinking that i might not
be what everyone here says they
know i am & that is why i can't
be trusted to tell anyone & even
you what you don't want to hear

SAD

For Stuart Barnes

IS ME
      not my style [?] me-
aning may you
      not suffer from TOO MUCH
tropical sleeping, or a lack
           of A or C or E or K or light like we
              have done HOT STUFF,
dinners and dictionaries, so dig big words
        into brains
           like nails into…and you
                too have to scratch
        at that mean bit
which shrieks *shadow*
           why do you forsake yourself?
TUFF TITTIES, so what
        is the cue for that disease? it's lit
        is
          -n't it? of course
not! E-NUFF! we'll borrow sorrow tomorrow

O

no, look, it's darkness indivisible, isn't it
so you talk to the sea, which shushes you up and makes
your spine hear the sky, and how language hides
ways to help, see, like when a baby cries
'AIR!' when it needs to burp, but it's no
surprise we've grown on our own
with a few hands to twist us so we shout and fit
or at least feel the bit that's harsh enough
to hold us on the land where we don't want to stay
so still or go this slow but we do, you know

Solo

'peace is plausible'
Sam Wagan Watson, 'the fatal garden'

dear me, don't you just go up & down
from the ground to the solar ceiling
& you suck at love like a tit on a figure
of eight lying sideways, playing at being
some sort of vanishing plant or stool-pigeon
when the light catches itself in its glass, laughing
what have i done to deserve such worth,
such crusty biscuit, such terrible glow?

the response is to be awake while asleep
in your dream, every single smidgeon
with its own original sound-track
but shit, jack, you sure know how to keep
your head on, & even though the stars
are blinking to show the whole one-house town
the way to go out of the sticks & into the pits
you're not lonely in your corner of infinity

E

i would rather be lying on my back, dreaming
while you do whatever you want

or typing senseless love-poems
onto your flesh

or even singing your praises
with my tongue inside you

but instead i have been staring a long time
at the doorway, wondering what to say next

Smoke & Ash

For Joni M and Glyn M

        take me out, leave me there.
        suck me in or breathe the air.

help yourself, first one's free.
drop me or keep me.

        light me up, put me out.
        learn to hate what need's about.

feel me burn, then stop me.
keep me, and drop me.

        give me up, and start again.
        choke a sob, make ache your friend.

find a way to beat me.
drop me then keep me.

Passed

    the heart is quicker than the mind, so
        when it rains, she sometimes feels
      like joining in, & then a pretty self-pity
          becomes a savage sadness

        then you adore her by not wanting to
but hurting, & fall headlong into too much
of a mirror—still you hold on
    & behold there a vision as dark as a pupil

trapped within six walls, an itch becomes a rash
    & her spirit crawls & caws like a crippled crow

then, finally, tired by the shadows in the shadows
    in the seasons of her day, she hurtles
down & down through the ancient cracks
    into a brief & cacophonous doze

Sepia

everything beginning again to be
                covered in the slightest of dusts
        being blasted by the ragged
            restless winds which rattle the back
    door sending dried-out winter leaves
          and insects flying past
the weeks-old smoke hazing the horizon
              turning the light through
closed windows
         and the view outside already
            into memories of the days
      we were sleepier and the time before
the real fires came

Don't

don't
don't go
don't go away
don't go away again
don't go away again please
don't go away again please don't
don't go away again please don't go
don't go away again please don't go away
don't go away again please don't go away again
don't go away again please don't go away again please don't
don't go away again please don't go away again please don't
don't go away again please don't go away again please
don't go away again please don't go away again
don't go away again please don't go away
don't go away again please don't go
don't go away again please don't
don't go away again please
don't go away again
don't go away
don't go
don't

Eclipse

in an unreal glass, i eyeball myself
snoring in the shadow of a warning

i was her april fool for a year or two
like the masterpiece left in a dream

you seek the secret of your desires
where that flour flowers into bread

now dawn arrives slow as a window
& a mad dragon swallows the moon

the skyscrapers are like tombstones
the wind points the way to the future

Fourteen Paces

Da   some things you have to stand up for
my daughter playing the piano in my imagination
full of it, really—really, full
there it is, birth, and the return to the earth
birds go twittering all around
drank the beer just because it made me feel good
and better that than to snort and vamoose
you take the little thing at times and hope for the best
you'd do it with your foot just to save from bending over
knew a nap would be needed, though
ah, but it's not always peaceful in the country
nope, the same job again and again
grass the colour of cheap bread, and most
other folks white like our lies

See   over there, sir, it was him
no, me, i swear
i was trying to work
or not weep or err
didn't ignore your advice
for a minute, sir
was just hoping to remember
exactly what the words were

sadder about it than you, sir
but must admit you're right
i do have a tendency to be a bit of a dreamer
and oh yes, that's so true
Every animal knows how to hide.
i wrote it five hundred times

Piece

yes, some nights i'd rather make poetry
than love, like you prefer sun-showers
to a nice hot bath with perfectly placed
candles & a copy of 'the writing of the
disaster' to last you through the decade.
so after i've cleaned my cage & fed the
plants & the birds, then i can have a big
stretch, & a cup of something soothing
though at times it's about as pleasing as
a piece of pus & i end up feeling as rich
as a fly & as loving as a rained-on bone.
failure teaches one fine lesson, though—
if you must have bitterness, don't drink
it on the run, or even when slightly cold.

Old Spice

days like these you smell a lot like a goat
you dream of stealing from beggars
but really you can only go where you're driven to

at least twenty-one times a week spices are the spice of life
and you live with the pain that backs up into your brain
from trying to forget so much blood under the bridge

you bleat like a baby who can swallow almost anything
and admit, too, that you're as sad as a late-night train
or the last eight or nine prime ministers

though everyone says you write nearly as well as leonard
lennon
you just want to get on with your friends' directions
but you're about as able as an unstable table in a fable
so go, go and find the way to get away with calling
your latest collection 'Poems Old & Neglected'

The Dark

i need just a minute
to leave you my mark,
so will you permit me
to speak of the dark?

i've spent enough time there
to cheat you with lies—
but why should i hide
what is seen beyond eyes?

laid out in my bed
where the night was least bright,
i would try to bargain
with the demon of night.

while the smallest of shadows
shook encouraging fists,
i would offer my heart
to his laughing black lips—

until dawn made him shrink
past what could be perceived—
then the help would arrive,
and i'd leave.

COLLIDE

*'For less than a second / Our lives will collide /
The endless suspended / The door open wide'*

Leonard Cohen, 'The Book of Longing'

The Dark Site

cannot escape the hand that hurts
and the murk swarms
into your mouth
like a liquid mirror
in the care of your enemies' masters

they take their enhanced techniques
and insure they infect you everywhere
and the disease screams and shrieks
and you beg for dreamless sleep

there are detailed manuals prepared
for the interrogation
of those like us
and we sing the imperfect symmetry
of our songs of love to the air
whose mad and inescapable name is
'security'

Four Paces

Adios

```
somehow you manage to keep not dying, so beg
another chance to bow down before whatever
stops you from being unlucky again
         you know we're all tethered to this
here in the ether, trying not to dream like a pain
called home, where the unfamiliar faces of the big
lords on the lookout prove you can never go where?
to that hemisphere of midnight hair?
     so (something close to the littlest hobo)
you gotta go on trotting down the road, real slow
     & stay true & behoved to the thing
that is your squishiest ripest fig, dig?
i knew you'd understand, but we both smile in fear
of being misdiagnosed or believed in too much
```

Lo

```
              hello autumn my old foe
just thought i'd see how you're holding up and what
     do you do but return my gentle gaze with eyes of flesh
and that's when i fall into old ways of locking both doors
                and drinking the first one fast
                and an itchy scratch stretches out
          inside that can only be reached with that
             stillness that wilfulness that lack
of temperamental illness which is found when one makes
either the two of 'that' or 'this' into none
because every sunday i'm a mass of self-pity
                    to be dealt with—if only
there was a way to the soul that's not through the body
     is there?                    show me.
```

Ick   There Is Something Terribly Wrong With Me.
Of Course. With You.
I Am Terrified Of Death.
But I Am Far Too Fond Of Dry White Wine.
And The Next Morning Every Angle
Is Terrible, Or At Least Quite Often.
Yes, Too Many Repetitions Is The Problem
With People. Terrifying, Aren't I?
I Sure Need A Hair Doctor.
You See, You Know You Can Really Get
Rewarded For Regurgitation.
And Often It's, It's, It's Good Enough
Fun. Especially When One Is Unwell,
Or On The Side Of Caution. Yay!

Cake   waking to the gloom mostly without alarm
but still can't afford to burn the toast
instead, you make a cake with layers of betrayal
as everyday as wednesday
        this old man is close to holy
        with the precious memories of a terrier
        the only safe place is on top of the heater
        and in summer they call the weather 'fine'
we signed up in pencil with the other pleasure-soldiers
you fought the wall, and of course the wall won
now you chortle like a camel in a swamp
it was a love that grew like mould
        throw aside these words like a promise
        sometimes you're sad, you were had

Specks

they throw their money onto his blood
the rich ones exit through the entrance

she hit me from behind but i managed
to miss the brick wall & keep on flying

he asked 'is it tomorrow or yesterday?'
then played peek-a-boo with her heart

we're crying our tears into a rising sea
the guardians of confusion scope it all

words kiss words so you pocket them
in the long run you hope you can walk

We Were Made

we
were
made to
make & maybe
above all to make
love & to make each
other over & over & again
as if we were waves falling
onto themselves &
we were falling
into ourselves
towards where
we come
from

Loses

      what? turn off the news
    at least—only the names get rearranged,
and we can sit down and have one of those
soothing beverages. everything reeks
    of smoke, and some strange
chemical i don't know the number of.

distances have disappeared. we should
    be fine; our plans will save us,
and those who aren't obviously weren't.
somewhere else someone might lose
some things, but shut up, ok...anyhow,
    if the wind changes,
your face will stay like that.
      come on, deep breaths now.

Please Do

how dare you be bored! let's dress up naked
        & we can splash around in the tides
of some turbulent euphoria, or at least let me take
my pencil & tease the tip of the top of your top lip

i'll write something there to tickle all your funny-bones
      i'll touch you like pouring water into a glass
  you do that thing where you smother me in otherness
& i'll sharpen my teeth on the delicate veins of your wrists

  then we can do something more serious or even sillier
like perfecting our skills in scorpio-scopophilia

  i know i've got a thin chin & i can't maintain the wage
but don't tick me like a list, i promise i'm a believer
in not leaving, i'll be a comrade in your arms
  i can be silent forever, & i'll meet you where you are

Episodes

                i who am mostly free
                think of the ways i am not free

becoming transparent
made her invisible

                at the cliff's edge
                push comes to shove

the storm came into the room
so he stopped his sobbing

                the link broke, we quickly
                were a joke

over the phone, she tells him
i'm sorry, i'm an office all day

                i sing to the birds
                but i make sure no one hears

Loose Ideas

that the same questions return like water and its murmur
it's undeniable as a future of untraceable erasure

and that she could be doomed by one futile flaw
she might never see until she's hiding at death's door

and also that though i'm nothing like a hero or a nought
there are still so many things i insist on not being taught

so how many abstractions can fit inside a poem this size
when you can't even step into the same bath twice?

My Daughter at One Hundred Months

need a nurture-needle because of all the love
i fling at you and how your voice
is as flat as white bread and your distant
head droops like a bent bookmark but you have to
wonder am i meant to be meaningful anyway
when i'm shivering here in an image's shadow

just felt a small call well up from within so had to
be the glad dad and tap into the thing
and send it with big smiles and lots of kisses
now i've got my sun to go brown in and my heart
is as large as a tear thinking of you sitting there
staring at something as plain as all the broken lines

K

are we in greedy agreement, or do i say i do
not go along with that law, big daddy, and i
mean it, 'cos a childish dream is an endless
need, and you better beware, get ready, my
soul-twin is a bear named teddy, but he can
buy you fine ice or repossess your screams
with the powers of his cousins and his claws
so how you gonna do your time? yo, when
i grow up i'll throw trees around like knives

Dole

'If you use language, I'm going to work.'
The Boys [dir. Rowan Woods, wri. Stephen Sewell/Gordon Graham]

        so much time, and so little money to waste
but plenty of pleasure from most of the free things
which are, of course, most of the best things
all the same, i can't forget the hidden ones—you know the ones
i mean, the ones who are laughing at us, no, they barely think
of us, other than when we fail to serve them appropriately
                i tell you though, friend, deep
in the brutal gloom of the sewers
where their own origins may well have been
a stench is beginning to arise that even we
        cannot bear, and in a little while, maybe in
my lifetime, when that stink rises to the level of the street
    and we manage to forget the priceless cheapness
of most our art and our sport, we will find our meekness
      has spilled over, and our justice, merciful and ripe
will be doled out to those ones who have caused the most grief

D

Kelpie

when you come home each night i just want to lick your face gotta slurp up that regurgitated goodness from your guts yep though i know everyone here is above me & you're the boss of 'em all & if i'm as honest as they say i am what i have to admit is i just want to run after you or whatever it is you say i should run after & then i get to do your dirty work for you i'll make those stupid animals disappear like ex-boyfriends & that guy who hangs around he wouldn't even know what service looks like i'm the one who can really give you what you need ok i'm sorry i'll shut up now & just lie at your feet

Poodle

yes well we both know i want to be your dog but you have to admit it certainly pleasures you greatly to gaze at me like i'm the one who is the king of tricks & being clever even though certainly there are things you can do that maybe i can't but so what i can make you laugh any time i want & you can never do that to me though most of the time i'm smiling quietly at myself & my genius at playing jokes because isn't that really what it's all about no you don't think so please permit me if i may to show you a few things about my rigorous knowledge of myself & what you strange beings think truth seems to be

Seidel's

sidled up, said some fink
-ish thing re. rich bitches
including him
-self, made out
like he's lying in the shade with his self's other
otherness in a burn
-ished mirror, blown
all over the place in
-cluding is
-rael, wiped up the mess with
us, dropped
us in the re
-cycling re
-ceptacle, and just ad
-justed his dirty spectacles

ha we've gone
off home in a rage
where the living is cheesy inside a ho
-use with no shame
not suicidal but mad going you can
not be serious you'll never get
away with this you will
even though sometimes oddly neglecting to mention some
-thing irritatingly ex
-cluding of the poor bourgeoisie who even sometimes get
the joke's on us

Polis

'The metropolitics of globalisation will take over from the geopolitics of nations, just as the latter once took over from the city-state of the antique origins of politics.'
Paul Virilio, City of Panic

all crowns are built on carrion

        collude with yourself in a cheating-place

    most capitals are no longer animal-compatible

climate change is returning us to our origins

      a poet is an exile from the main street

too much art leads to paper windows

      plastic bags will last longer than humanity

          you can't argue with excreta

60 gigahertz is a killer

      we are quiet where grass grows over our eyes

putrefaction purifies

Close

eye, you have grown tired of me
looking over and above
so you have to close and open
to shut this trap up again

the night is full of rustling rats
the digital clock blinks once a minute
and i'll die a few dozen deaths in hope
the ache won't outlive the week

yes, yes, you already told me
you can read me like a crook
you can't leave the future, so let me go
and re-write the old lines of my leaving

but what you forget is i'm just
like the sun or a cobra, in that
if you want to see me up nice and close
i'm afraid you have to stop breathing

Id

'true revolution / comes from true revulsion'
Charles Bukowski, 'the people'

yawning as i tell my nightmare
               they always end the same
           like the edible flesh of the neck
     as if you only have two rooms to live in
         this shining thing has its twin where i frown
    and still i need the sun too much like a pansy
alright then a sunflower, but not hurrying the squinting or flourishing
  all i do in forests is get lost
or find a charred man called carl drinking cabbage tea
              and he's chanting 'something will defeat you'
         so much i want to throw out
the past keeps rising from the holes in the floor
              i stared into her as if she was an open fire
but sometimes too soon the lust turns to rust
            and then you learn the smart ways
to ignore the trillionaires who chortle like hyenas
and the tongues that grumble 'too late'
    quick let's love each other before we fall in the grave

Repeat After Me

no way at all there's too much of everything
your inside is out and your outside is in and
the great australian dream is smaller than us
but there's nothing new here other than fun
i'm wrong i'm wrong i'm wrong i'm wrong
sorry, i can't help you i'm just doing my job
now noting knowing nothing noting nothing

i must do something about this terrible mess
o great man you are such a wondrous writer
yes your messiah-complex is so enthralling!
let's go and compare the size of our idiocies
party dude party dude party dude party dude
we did not come from apes are we not men?
no it's not our problem, it's not our problem

Adolesce

still at that dreamy stage where
the days have become decades
& one finally begins
to comprehend the truth of being
alone, facedown in the hospital
doing my best to keep you in my
heart, hypocrite lecturers & fans
of perpetual air-conditioning, sour
cream, & conservative governments
but my mind's not right or left
it's more akin to windscreen-wipers
in a bomb i can't remember the model or
year of, in an underground car-park in the desert
with the radio just able to pick up
the last non-screening talkback station left
which i've strangely called & am on hold to
& the waiting music is something resembling
'greensleeves' played by a machine from june 1982
it's all about the timing, how one follows each
like the same thing & the good gaga google-goons go
goo-goo over & over about it & share there, natch
& you don't want to be left all alone, well maybe

Lies

                there's really no choice

all men are meant to be mended

    the nose is not the most powerful organ

         you and i will be remembered

    the prostitute won't swallow for the prosecutor

he has the perfect sincerity of a man who has convinced himself of the truth

                flattery will get you nowhere

                  i know what i'm talking about

                    a paradox can't be true

                      no harm in trying

        egg yolks are yellow and white folk are white

                          my feelings get in the way of my real feelings

          you are not a unique snowflake

no humans were harmed in the making of this poem

                      sorry, but i'm cursed

KID D

'Let's hear it for the vague blur!'
Richard Linklater [wri. /dir.], A Scanner Darkly

it's a messy weekend's piss-weak end
                         and, man, we're as crazy as soldiers in here
            bingeing's a solo sport, but you took one for the team
     liver barely living, heart cracked open wide
              from the faults put in there

another fair-weather lover runs to their absent father
       and one more bottle hits the bottom
of where the chemicals are taking you, so you prop
             and try not to shut the shutters on your youth
the planet goes so fast it sometimes seems to be gone

                listen, most of us are dead air
and the expiring get less respect than the perished, but hey
       no drama, llama-farmer, it's late, we're all freakin' sinkin'
                    gotta raise the bar lower!
     you think you'll never love like this again, and you're right

Idol

you do not work you
only play & eat nothing
that was
angry or scared
you speak
only when something
speaks in you
otherwise you sleep & love
yourself becomes you

Solid Case

the whirring machines start up again. his finger accidentally touches the wrong bit of the screen. again. it's three o'clock for the three hundredth time, so in a brief fistic farce, he hits himself in the face repeatedly, but he doesn't want to die. he often gets confused about his direction in life, especially how he should go about his career goals—centrifugal or centripetal? either way, all will be well. snow nearly always goes all the way to the fence, but the lightning bolt is rarely before the storm.

in this covert kingdom here, the lords are not, sadly, not lauded. he sees himself as the greatest of the solar worshippers, the greatest of them all, but it can be an issue in winter. one is always, always punished for one's weaknesses, always, and that makes you go, 'OW, STOP HURTING ME!' you get past the point pretty quickly, and that's the point of brevity and discipline, right? you get to the holy days quicker, and then you can keep staring through a spider's web mandala and transcending stuff.

can you keep a secret, though?

Thank You for Letting Me Be Someone Else Again

i'd never been more caught and felt so free
i can't tell lies so i'll say it this way
she was a messenger from the mystery

sometimes i forgot which of one of us was me
when we were touching and all thought fell away
i'd never been so caught and felt more free

i sang clichés like a bird in a tree
and smiled like a buddha on christmas day
she was a messenger from the mystery

her heart spoke tricks i could never foresee
our house was the stage for a badly made play
i'd never been so caught and felt more free

even young lovers can't always agree
how to laugh and let skies fall where they may
she was a messenger from the mystery

may we all always gaze with eyes that see
may i never despise the places i stay
i'd never been more caught and felt so free
she was a messenger from the mystery

If You Go Away

or the way he points the way to outrageous wealth
metaphors, one cannot deviate from it, still
i can't compete, no, i'm fine like darwin, and anyway
i've been told i'm worth my weight in cardamon,
then she said 'someone's
got to give', but i brushed her off
like a bug on a title page,
actually the biggest cockroach you've ever seen.
see, pain-killers don't kill it, they just go
to sleep with you finally to be wished
upon a star, or like jogging on bonito flakes
at altitude in heat without crushing
your expectations or those of opposing fans
just waiting, watching you redden your neck
for the great southern chopping block,
but your brain's not as sweet as a big glass jar
of organic dried figs, though it resembles a walnut,
or even the way dark turned off
gets lighter and is never black enough.
shit, he gives me a shame-headache, and my base is sore.
leave me just enough glove
and don't become who you aren't.

Disclose

in the desert
when it rains there
it falls everywhere
and then the starved earth
lets its hidden gifts appear

allow me to do to you
what that water does
so that we might learn
some of the secrets
our bodies disclose

Clap

i hear you, it's contagious
    this love
            thing, this urge to shape
            and be remade, i tell you outrageously unnecessarily

again, the fingers are restless tonight, the drums
                        in the heart send out
impressively-coded signals to all the bases
            hope i can put them where they'll do some good

        so off you go, skipping like a puppy
            towards a glimpse of new tricks
and you'll sit up and lie down and shake hands and play dead
to get your big bickies and a bone

rough, this need to be heeded
    to tell truth to the powerful-in-theory
            to leave a scent to be traced and erased, like all of us
who swagger in, and stagger out

        somewhere it's written and repeated 'there are
no refunds', and when you're done touching yourself to death
        you'll leave a fine mess, then one more time
you'll pull yourself together and your hands apart

Disease

like you, i'm afraid
of being wrong
& of having gone
too far from where i belong

i don't know anymore
how to see
inside to the centre
of what i could be

my mouth is open
but my heart can't hear
for the hurt in my guts
that grows from year to year

Minimal Characters

the woman with the beautifully-formed eyes

the omega male

the bribed and smiling journalist

the gentleman who only worships the whore of horror

the trampled jockey

the wealthy widow who argues in her sleep

the arrogant sage

the one who has to be moved by crane

the broken-eyed jeweller

the one who put the 'i' in 'spied'

the boy who is always sorry

the vicious christian

the fly-eater

the shadow laughing in a doorway

When I Knew

it was over

i sat
in the kitchen
sobbing beyond pride
but still afraid
of the image
i knew i appeared to be

what i was
could not stay
within any longer

so like a man

i begged her
for a cuddle
and like a young slave
she told me
she didn't have
time

Speed

a past oral, sham glam of how once you're in
your 40s you start forgetting how old you are
to relive the halcyon days of the cellophane cudgels' first
lp which is actually still kinda cool like the moon in a spoon
or yeppoon in june, or merely by recalling
ancient masters drinking straight
from their cupped palms while imperturbably
betraying their complete lack of geographical knowledge
gee, wow, now we hunch over these little palm-offs like
we're looking for the ocean in a bottle, but when cometh
the hour to actually stop fidgeting & own up
to what we could have done, it's a hubbub of static-fluff
we're as dumb as a baby's bum, yup
you lose you strain you stay on the plain where all
the future ripples before you like an inland lake
of a trillion dollars' worth of fifty-cent pieces hey
didn't-you-hear-me-for-fuck's sake
-turn-that-shit-down-i-can't-bear-black-sabbath
-or-bartok-or-whatever-it-is at least i worked
for a living once you smart-mouth prick

Sacked

ease, as if a slow breeze
floats across me, loosely
staring at a not-especially
ugly mark on the wall

outside, children are chuckling
& the grown-ups try to grow things

the day is cool, the sheets are warm
my aches are resting quietly

was it really that i quit my own
rat-trap, & how many times
will this freedom astonish me
once more before i die?

i roll over, lie on my back
not even needing to smile
& in the bottom of my tea cup
a garden begins

Cool

the chill of the rain disabuses one still human of any further

sitting
so it lifts
itself
and steps
over
puddles
as if an
ordinary
dancer
taking
care
not to
fly
away
or forget
to hold
its spine
straight &
umbrella
overhead

water's
so wet
but
the bridge
is not
underwater
yet

Docile

might as well
have one more shot

i don't really feel it
even though it's hot

and though i know
i'm nothing that i've got

it's new year's eve
but i pretend that it's not

A-Sides

For Forbes

for now i'm older than you
ever were, and can tell
someone that while you went back
there to die, i got out of the deep south just
before some life-affirming pump packed it
in, and for this kid, the kidney is key
not that i believe in 'em, but
what were yours? the back
door was always left open
in the days before expensive drugs
and children or singles were easily left
with their slowly-liberating mothers
i'd like to chuck
you out with the bong-water, but you stay
'round like a good bad cough at 45
teaching us with girth by sea
of the way through the Heads as yours, or
how you said 'others have armchairs
& opinions about things', how happiness
should wear its talent, or how the past will
be, or even how you like what you have
because Nothing Succeeds like Egress
to make you go back
to the start, correct, daddy-o?

How Low Now

        drinking in the pits of bitterness
making friends with hate and gettin' matey with death

                      a low-down lay-down
                close to closed

    like light fading through faded curtains
can no longer assent to the yes-men in my head

        she couldn't sleep in a grave
                all the invisible gray children

      solutions have so much to answer for
but does the heart really lie on the left?

              a numb mumbling doubly done
think i'll stick my tongue through you

        let me revise that silence
it's never ending, so i started it again

Oops

me is so interesting
    you are too, i'm enchanted
        and i promise to tell the truth
like a diagonal dude prancing over cracks in a hailstorm
    but, gee, i don't want to hit the nail off the thumb
    we all do our best, isn't that right
    but now the earth turns black
like a giant eyeball that's stared too long at itself
    and you go on and on and on about it
though it's never long enough
        me, too, i could have done more
    but i is an author

As

raw as war
as rich as air

as true as blues
as new as news

as near as never
as far as ever

as old as night
as cold as i

Tough Thought Throughout Though

you win the toss, though kindly offer me the break.
make no mistake, that's where your luck will break.

though i'm the inferior craftsman, and a bit
of a fool by far, i can easily snort and break

into the grin of such a tough-guy thug that every pair
of sockets i look upon pleads 'please give me a break!'

you can't be tricked at all, though, you know
too much of the cracked places the heart can break,

and the ways, too, it hurts the organs if the poet
hasn't thought through where the line should break.

the drummer in the corner, though, sends precision out
and all the funky lovers nodding, dancing to the break.

april's not the coolest month, but it's tough not to groove
even when your back is asking for a toilet break.

look, matt, mate, don't lose it, but the thought remains
that promises and winning streaks were made to break.

Space

i went out into cold, radiant space
that realm where oceans dance unseen
and you brush zones of recognition
that will linger as enigma

there the night is that immense it's like a face
and there's so much sibilance inside the silence
it seems to be the beginning of the need to make
where all your wishes are quivering in stillness

you drift through fruitless gardens
of your own hushed yearnings
like breezes searching for the easefulness of lakes
or a giant bug looking to touch the earth

now every evening i thank the nearest star
that i was made to burn so fast
that i was cursed with this great birth
and that tomorrow never goes

Dick

For Sacha Baron Cohen

he thinks i believe him
        which is very much
                to my advantage

                when he talks
                & i'm smiling, he thinks
                        he knows why

he is sure of his power
        which makes him softer
                & that means danger

                i was never a believer
        in his unholy war
but now i am even wiser

                he thinks i am still
        an idiot, but he's wrong—
                me, i am a fool

I

    think they said i got away with words
                      me being me
he sells himself like a clapping seal
    tried to cut my childhood in half
sucked and swallowed, mornings full of night
        strangest knife i've ever known
            as fast as the last
your face was an eye i saw through
          mirrors glancing, did i kill something?
when your hopes become rain on the roof
      ignore it
unknot the not
        now a lime tree grows inside me
  understanding i'm still standing still
        finders, weepers, losers, keepers
i'm no good in the way i get in the way of the good day
                    ah, the dirt of the clean break
my spleen keeps falling out my mouth
           cowards go first
                        lost in the cosmos
  i offer a free eyelid turn-down service
     ignore it
      spots on my hands and spots on the sun
        you were as close to my heart as the inside of my nose
     now our hearts are asleep in our heads
inflexible neck of time
   i will behead you
     then i'll slide these letters under your door

OK

    computers can't compete with an old bloke
clad well, grant me that much, at least, & he's got
      the know-how, & lying in a drawer at home
a t-shirt which says in a large-impact font
      GIFTED LIVER, but more power to him & his gang
    i say, they're still working the net & the angles
& putting it out as easily & happily as 3-year-olds dance
in 4-dimensional poems about fisher-king heroes
      it's as plain as pain & even more
joyous than the void, this life-sized chunk
of pulp fiction with your name on the inside
        this thing you can look up
to, too, almost a flamboyance of flamingoes
        it's better than great, it's alright

Inside Out

to get on the inside
it turns on itself

turns in
on the outside

turns itself
off inside

to get outside in
around and round it turns

Afterword

Below are some ideas that informed this book, and if there's a motto for the collection, this would do it: '*IN GIRUM IMUS NOCTE ET NOCTE ET CONSUMIMUR IGNI*' [Anon. referred to by Guy Debord et al, and translated roughly as 'we turn in a circle in the night and are consumed by fire'.]

'The radical online news outlet *Mada Masr* recently published an article on the coping mechanisms deployed by journalists, activists, artists, human rights workers and scholars: 'For those who see themselves as connected to the revolution, but remain [in Egypt],' the piece noted, 'these are depressing times, and increasingly lonely times too, as friends and comrades leave or are imprisoned.' It posed the question: 'What do you do to get through?' Among the answers from readers were colouring books, computer games, knitting, kaleidoscopes, drinking, drugs and dancing.'
Jack Shenker, 'Coming Home to the Counter Revolution'

'Ours is indeed an age of extremity. For we live under continual threat of two equally fearful, but seemingly opposed, destinies: unremitting banality and inconceivable terror. It is fantasy, served out in large rations by the popular arts, which allows most people to cope with these twin specters.'
Susan Sontag, 'The imagination of disaster'

'It is therefore, in some sense, the poverty of the world of technology that is its truth, and its great—intellectual—virtue is not to enrich us but to denude us. A barbarous world, without respect, without humanity. It empties us horribly of everything we love and love to be, drives us from the happiness of our hideouts, from the semblances of our truths, destroys that to which we belong and sometimes even destroys itself. A fearsome test. But this contestation, precisely because it leaves us destitute of everything except power, perhaps also gives us the chance that accompanies any rupture: when one is forced to give up oneself, one must either perish or begin again; perish in order to begin again.'
Maurice Blanchot, 'Man at Point Zero' [trans. Elizabeth Rottenberg]

'The merit of style exists precisely in that it delivers the greatest number of ideas in the fewest number of words.'
Viktor Shklovsky, *Theory of Prose*

'You will never be able to tell me why you exist but you will always be ready to maintain a serious attitude about life. You will never understand that life is a pun, for you will never be alone enough to reject hatred, judgements, all these things that require such an effort, in favour of a calm and level state of mind that makes everything equal and without importance.'
Tristan Tzara, 'Lecture on Dada' [1922]

'Everything is broken up / & dances'
Jim Morrison, 'Far Arden'

'Art is [...] mobilized, not because it has worth in and of itself, or with an imitative and cathartic aim, but to raise the void of Truth up to the point at which dialectical sequential linking is suspended.'
Alain Badiou, *Manifesto for Philosophy*

'This is why I sometimes characterize Badiou's philosophy as a 'SLAP philosophy': philosophy not only integrally relies on Science, Love, Art and Politics, but it gives you a slap to awaken you from the nightmare of history.'
Justin Clemens, 'Had we but worlds enough, and time, this absolute, philosopher...'

'art [...] proceeds in this way by successive destructions. To the extent that it liberates libidinal instincts, these instincts are sadistic.'
Georges Bataille, quoted in Frances Stracey, *Constructed Situations*

'So that we look at it with pleasure, look // At it spinning its eccentric measure. Perhaps, / The man-hero is not the exceptional monster, / But he that of repetition is most master.'
Wallace Stevens, 'Notes Toward a Supreme Fiction'

Acknowledgements

My thanks to all the editors who published a number of these poems (some in earlier forms) in the following publications, e-zines, and anthologies:

Abridged (NIR), *Australian Poetry Anthology*, *Bareknuckle Poetry*, *Bill Poetries*, *Burrow*, *The Canberra Times*, *Cordite*, *foam:e*, *fourW*, *Furiously Knocking*, *Giant Steps*, *Mascara Literary Review*, *Mod-Piece*, *MoTHER [has words]*, *Northerly*, *Prayers of a Secular World*, *pressure gauge*, *Shots from the Chamber*, *Spoken In One Strange Word*, *Teesta (IND)*, *Today*, *the voice you speak with may not be your own*, *The Tundish Review*, *Well-Known Corners*.

A number of poems have been broadcast on the television show *Red Lobster* [Channel31], and on the radio show *Spoken Word* [3CR].

Thanks to the Wheeler Centre, Melbourne, and their assistance in the writing of this book with a 'Hot Desk' Fellowship through Melbourne P.E.N in 2012.

Kaleidoscopic thanks to Shane Strange for all his work on this collection, and to Ali Alizadeh, Stuart Barnes, Brett Hetherington, and Nathan Shepherdson, who all read longer versions of this book, and gave much-needed critique. Ongoing gratitude also goes to those who have helped with my many aspects of my writing, particularly Owen Bullock, Grant Caldwell, Coral Carter, Jennifer Compton, Ange Cook, Karen Dawson, Bronwyn Evans, Nola Firth (and all the members of the Murbah workshop group), Dave Hatch, Joel & Ron Hetherington, Miles Du Heaume, Andy Jackson, Myron Lysenko, Simon Munro, and Melinda Smith.

Matt Hetherington has lived on Bundjalung country in the Northern Rivers region of New South Wales since 2016. He also makes music under the name ZAZIZ. www.matthetherington.net

www.ingramcontent.com/pod-product-compliance
Lightning Source LLC
Chambersburg PA
CBHW020327010526
44107CB00054B/2009